BLACK
HORSE
RUNNING

*A Collection of haiku,
tanka & haibun*

Clare McCotter

 Alba Publishing

Published by Alba Publishing
P O Box 266, Uxbridge
UB9 5NX, United Kingdom
www.albapublishing.com

A catalogue record for this book is available from the British Library

ISBN: 978-0-9551254-6-1

Edited, designed and typeset by Kim Richardson
Cover image © Victoria and Albert Museum, London
Printed by Ashford Colour Press, UK

10 9 8 7 6 5 4 3 2 1

Acknowledgements

Some of the haiku, tanka, haibun and poems in this volume originally
appeared or will be appearing in the following journals: *Blithe Spirit,
Presence, Haiku Scotland, Shamrock, Frogpond, The Heron's Nest, Modern
Haiku, Roadrunner, Simply Haiku, World Haiku Review, Acorn, Contem-
porary Haibun Online*, and *Paper Wasp*.

Contents

for judas
5

changing fields
13

soul bird
23

crumbs for the starlings
32

horse dream
41

only the magnolias
53

twins
60

jesus in indigo
70

In memory of Michael Lowery

stag with autumn cud
sapid reliquary
dark green memories

        dusky river
        swimming in pink sky
        the dog otter

rebel in russet
urban fox sashaying
down a cantaloupe moon

        reminding her why
        she is here
        a bolt of blackbird

stony beach
silver in a wolf moon
sheep bones

starlight
on leaf mulch
a worm's crystal pulse

enfolding
the fallen foxglove
a slug's soft dream

gravel path
silking the night
crossing rat

evening star
a silver sapling
in the junkyard

frozen fields
star dies
a horse sighs

taking him back
to the war
brown butterfly

slipper moon
shimmying black rock
the glass eel

the crooked sunflowers
at her wake
crayoned get well card

cemetery gate at dusk
old friend
no need to ring first

weeds on her grave
solo
a viola's velvet face

headstone in moonlight
my problems
still keeping you awake

sound of her voice
on snow
blue cedar shadow

veridical silver fish
slashing my bowl of night
meteorite

sparkling still
below a sky of starfish
the ct scanner

crescent moon
behind cloud cover
the barmaid's bruised eye

her cuban heels
among slippered souls
early dementia

dawn breaking
into the dark dream house
a finch's song

black fish nets
circling the crowded café
her sad trumpet

day moon
in the snow angel's heart
a sparrow

for judas

as their sandals mark the hill's warm side
quivering olive leaves silver the dry ebony air
only silver here not already transmuted into
hanging branch and field of blood but now
alone like him among judean stone and stars
my flushed mouth is a flower broken cen-
turies before in a prophet's white hand for
how could I not love this man and there was
night in the garden

tulips
incarnadine
his lips

falling star
starshaped space
miscarriage

                    angel wings washed
                    at dusk
                    an infant's grave

closed again
in the absence of wind
smooth urn

                    can you receive letters
                    over there
                    frost on a wild red rose

the sexton in silence
this evening will
come late
for a swallow nests
among the saints

moon burial

night in arabia as a turtle leaves the waves for the
first time in three years—slummocking sand to
space becoming womb she wraps her clutch in an
other dark and rows beach back to the salamstone
shallows a slow departure studied by strangers
from a distant land among them those who call
chelonia mydas an unfit mother but deep in sway-
ing sea grasses her sloe eyes know someday in
open ocean a silken shelled harvest will grow

social services
say adoption is best
valentine's day

starlit stilettos stepping
on every crack ...
how young she looks

           well water
           shed with red leaves
           her face

alone in the dunes
sky reflecting
my dog's cataract

           a gannet
           lost in dark sapphire
           her limp

maiden name
in the round gold moon
a frozen fern

           forty seven
           and no pension
           all the starry heavens

changing fields
for phil mccotter

it is summer and we are driving cattle through the gold
dusk behind slow swinging rumps a girl's sandals pool
charcoal in the ground mist of their breath as she directs
a ringle-eyed collie to a slap in the hedge couchant he
waits while the rough rattle of hooves pass impatience
or the wolf spurring him to nip the last and as they break
into an awkward trot you shout from the front to take
things easy the road to new grass is long and dry a
lintwhite moon already looms high when you open the
gate to your six acres our best field in the girl's eyes a
sea of pristine green now on this pavement where no
tracks mark the dark patina of dust it is summer and we
are driving cattle through the gold dusk

silent night
cattle on low land
archipelago

white wrists rinsed in a dead seal's eyes winter moon

violet night lamplighted lucent wings

three heavy horses in rape where I can not stop

the blue beyond broken ties a wishing kite

an unforgotten hand alone in damask dark a swan

in sleep still a dancer deep iris sky

rose dawn pulled tight around the bagwoman's shoulders

full in azure weather the condemned cow's udder

horse dream

chestnut mare you carried me to this land where cities are
coloured viridian and all our roads are water—cool opulent
ovals under apah animate lustral lapping baptising perfectly
russet hocks your forehead's crooked star sinking over my
unfolded palm a salfay of serafina and siberian blue smooth
on your sovereign tongue

summer dusk
a horse's soft mouth
feeding hands

blue roses
dying in their sleep
her secrets

        white crocus
        the pianist's trembling
        translucent hand

honey bee
feeding
at the mouths
of violets
mother's
prayer book

        night storm
        glistening
        the dark iris

out of reach
for so long
the black thorn
a rose now
on her tongue

        palestinian moon
        rising above cloudcover
        silver cigarette foil
        in his hands transfigured
        to silver flower

night
a swan's wing
everything

        alone under a cortège
        of stricken stars
        what blow has kept
        the arctic swan
        from its frozen land?

moonlit
  driftwood
    wavespun
      swan

        rising from
        a black horse dream
        swan song

their high country's
dying year turns thoughts
to her own low indigo lands
where a man whispers
the names of swans

female blackbird

fastened at the throat with a sprent of dark stars
brown is the colour of my stalwart cloak if ever
there were a misnomer it is the alias I have
borrowed from an other—sans gold-kholed eye
sans funereal glitter I am and will remain beyond
the bounds of any name travelling through
amaranthine scapes unrecognised by all but the
rach bitch

unnamed bird
on the cold magnolia tree
song shadows

first frost
brimming my hands
a grey mare's breath

the horses are gone
tonight in the far fields
a single silver moth

starlight
though none are here
the scent of horses

narrow lapis lake
deeper than sky
pupil of a horse's eye

bay horse entering
the clearing
entering the moon

geranium sunset
through trailing mane
an old caravan

night recitals
in memory of katie mcgill

what would you have made of your funeral would
you have thought we should have said a word or
two or more for you recalling plush nights—moon
a pool of silver seeds rising in the alembic of your
voice as you told your nieces about the lady of
shallot her clouded eyes leaving a silent loom and a
lacquer of flaxen stars starlight moving like an old
queen's train through your flamenco hands where
we watched behind willow fans for the singing
boat's approach on slow streams through long fields
of rye and bearded barley—our lady weary long
before the dark in lancelot's dark hair split day clean
as a jay's wing

footfall
on fallen leaves
a traveller's moon

condemned to four grey walls and four grey towers
you knew shallot's story well and those of other
woman working in thread—saule's spectral fingers
on an scandinavian spindle—orihme crossing the
milk river japanese deity on a bridge of dark green
feathers—philomela the mute nightingale spinning
shuttle song her mouth a cup of carnelian and you
kilrea's own factory girl weaving strange colours
by night and day

morning star
gold stubble fields
the factory's stirring heart

our nights with you were a poetry of travel—cara-
vanserai in perfumed morning air—hard journey-
ing in high frozen lands—a rebellious departure
from tapestry and mirror as your jet ring eclipsed a
lord's wrath in a geometry of broken glass gleaming
the smallest hours while you placed our slippered
feet beside road signs one pointing south to akhir
an-nahr one flung to the far north where silica trans-
mutes to snow and white birds close shy garnet eyes
to the raven's nacreous miracle—grained auburn
oak the weft of your full throat a chinese goddess's
seamless robe standing on our distaff side what
curse unravelled it when you died—in yew shad-
owed noon we should have said a word or two or
more for you

wild geese
in a full gemini moon
her grave

red gold water
the trout's footprints
crossing a bedouin sun

at the burial a wasp
reminds me
of last night's dream

may meadow at dusk
red fox spancelled
to a frolicking shadow

nothing surprises at the zoo
only you
grey squirrel on ash branch

it is not the storm
in this black november night
that spooks the horses

the dead hare is gone
among hazel roots and stars
its imprint still warm

soul bird

I have tried to dream again the blue cave lake at the
bottom of your opium eyes the alaskan silence of
your slow wings the landscapes glimmering in the
souterrains of your hollow bone I do not believe in
the soul but if some high decree scripted in island
purple declared one necessary for the world I would
suggest you white bird

night
pale wing
longing

belemnites

this sea is a harp its beach schille deposits of
aeolian rhythms—sands where no sleep ever comes
for always further back we lie among the belem-
nites—old words wrapped in marl and stone their
sharp syllables still refracting lights on the western
shore—teveriyah lodestar where I sent a girl's
image on a silent journey white feathers falling
from her eyes the letters of a foreign alphabet
coloured with night and topaz in the legends of her
map

after the funeral
a creased postcard from the back
of mother's heart

hypnotist

dinah was singing *September in the Rain* down
empty early morning roads where I could not avoid
you the single arrhythmic thud your heart flailing in
beating hands when I lifted it off the road one black
implacable eye arresting in a tachycardic breast the
other a crimson-rimmed depression where an eye
had been then shocking in its regularity your heart
beat slowed and as I inhaled the perfect purple of
that fox glove pulse somewhere a lost rhythm re-
turned—later amid stainless steel and squat yellow
smells they pronounced your eye intact I insisted it
was gone could such a vacancy fill itself? were you
a miracle bird? they agreed to observe you until I
returned that evening to two eyes watching waiting
imminent release—an account to settle: one rowan
tree in the garden

song thrush
silent under juniper
fog thickens

clouds in a mare's eye the fracture beyond repair

moonlight on a zinc roof dereliction music

wild geese parting the blue northern yearnings

amid all the red ink a crane fly's wing

black horse running rolling away the stone

tattered hem of a wedding dress winter moon

the shadow crossing the bridge crossing her face

schoolyard gates boy and pit bull embrace

Zikaron

Under Galilean skies
nothing is divined
in cedar ash.
The fire's blue
phosphorescent ghost
rises with the child
in a poppy sun
where music from
her box-wood flute
is a silver salamander
tracing your outline.
Its closeness
an inscrutable sign.

Andenken

Hanging in the balance
between two seasons
Alioth, the black horse
crosses a gulf
of burnt sienna
where our talk of time
and travel
and all you wrote
in the south cloaks
my macadamia lawn
as it collects the blossoms
from your throat.

Ruuru

It is night on the edge
of the desert.
As earth contracts
things lose their names
in a maze
of insomniac stars.
Out here
the smoke from
our fires touch
before following
separate paths into
the imponderable dark.

Souvenance

Tonight I sleep
with the Arctic moth.
Its weight is two
crystalline hands
on my spine
as I face the mountain
where blood turns to sound
my words to amber
in your mouth.
Resurrected now
you stand in this present
luminous beyond
all hallucination.

a pigeon's purple throat
sunstroked on the ledge below
my unturned page

liturgy of stars
flickering noon pavement
a pigeon's feet

evening in the library
waiting with Freud
for the pigeons' return

techno speak
outside on blue iridescence
pigeons sleep

sunlit gothic arch
the theology of light
a pigeon's gold eye

after the holbein christ
dusk gathering on
a pigeon's gaunt breast

dreaming the book

the room's heart dark-seasoned under a star struck
cupola refracting the hunter and his dogs—glass
censer dispensing silent benediction: first snow
sky's augur of forgiveness falling whiter than ever
before through it I approach a desk of turkish oak
where his hands offer a manuscript of sixteenth
century verse all unread all miraculous in cerulean
and gold

dust motes
in a lexicon of light
the library's faded colours

whale rider

black angel of the northern wave far from warm
wintering waters your barnacled head bowed in
supplication fluked arms breaching sky—rorqual
acrobatics I lift from the wall only to abandon the
yellow duster for there behind the picture is a
butterfly of the night its closed wings a seamless
secret I am loath to touch in case touching crumbles
the perfect umber of this winter corpse but then
antennae stir and at my finger's faltering approach
sea smells rise in a spiral of brindled air—song of
the mottled moth alive on a baleen's tail alive in
this its true north

winter sea
flint in chalk cliffs
blue hieroglyphics

old medical notes
call him *imbecile*
when he thinks no one
is looking he spreads
crumbs for the starlings

outside her window
tall in dark sienna sky
the lightning tree …
tomorrow morning
electroconvulsive therapy

under low gentian hills
the lough is silver
as I drive home
from the asylum
from those brown eyes

as the mammogram
begins she gathers
a secret harvest—
rhododendrons
shedding scarlet

guttering votive candle in the wino's hand a butt

down here in different dark hard tracks

first scan head bowed over a tiny anemone hand

unmooned in the white woods a bird's wing

scarecrow's crucified arms hungry for some dark star

low over rose waters a heron

falling snow the child's hand full of sky

sickly wolf curled up in a doorway the drunk's tattoo

like himself
in memory of murt mcgill

with peaked cap hanging on the arm-rest you knelt every
morning your spare utilitarian frame almost invisible in
the back pew where graciously ushering opportunist
late-comers on past you stuck tight to the end of the seat
a quiet departure guaranteed

empty chapel
sunstrewn stained glass
a broken pieta

it is april murt and you are harnessing a bay clydesdale
which you did six mornings out of seven—tranced by
the burgundy tones of a voice you never raise he stands
with up-turned back hoof fly-flicking through half
closed eyes in a quarry at the round rocks—you loading
the high unsprung cart with material used to patch this
weave of local roads—your work in progress as the
done day sinks in low meadows

still ruby evening
the turn
of the sexton's key

soberly barred the only mount you owned a tall thin bi-
cycle gaunt and promising as a naked mast—in
bib and brace with shirt sleeves rolled up to the

elbows three open buttons airing the coarse white vest
you pedal steadily to the wolf island—turf spade
strapped to your sombre steed

leaden skies
a sparkle of sheared sheep
wondering why

passing tracks disused since 1952 you cross
mcfall's bridge then follow a rough rodden to the dark
heart there you stand at a moss bank tracing and back-
nicking the first layer of too-brown turf cutting and
lifting with slow methodical precision as you move
down to eye level—later four sandwiches wrapped in
waxen red and white loaf paper a lemonade bottle
filled with tea and one cigarette from a slim ten
pack—travelling home with the first star you push the
bike up mcwilliams' hill sunburnt and slightly
stooped—free wheeling to the road end

summer shower
hawthorn blossoms dripping
laudanum moon

scented and shrouded on white satin under the
scrutiny of a crucified jesus and a welcoming virgin
the snow fall of masses still to be said and there
against the wall that lean keen-eyed sentinel the cof-
fin's lid Murtagh on the name-plate *doesn't he look
like himself* soft on a neighbour's tongue

Souvenir

Glazed feathers warm
against my palm—
mythological bird
or rare pheasant from
a Benedictine garden
still among strange
weather as Paris
dawns oloroso
in the cup I stole
from a café
at Gare Du Nord.

Thakera

It is the aqua heart
of a Palestinian night.
Dust smells quiver
on the road to Qalqilya.
You do not speak
the white moon
is a frozen island
where our footsteps
leave no sound
and always
the orange trees.

where water turns to moon a hawthorn bows

if she had not stopped to pick the last pink rose

hoar frost on ploughed earth the moon's breath

along the margins of all soul's night tracks

velveting the derelict roof a patch of moon

starlight moving through the scent of horses

christmas moon on her grave white cyclamen

night frayed behind the purple pines a horse's call

Long-Stay

long-stay ward
a forged signature
on the mother's day card

depression
burned out cigarette
between her fingers

wind chimes tinkling
a key turns
in the asylum garden

long-stay ward
letters from long lost friends
in his own longhand

meteor shower
the self harm scars
gleaming her left arm

the asylum garden
summer breeze
rustling her rosary

long-stay ward
an old man's tense jokes
faecal incontinence

schizophrenia
stain on the beige shirt
he will not change

the asylum's lawns
a blue plume
of homing pigeons

long-stay ward
toothless half-moon smile
sly medicine spoon

stabilised psychosis
home
without any voices

the asylum clock tower
in evening sun
one white pigeon comes

long stay ward
the name unknown
on a mother's day card

earth raven

dreaming the full span of your candescent wings a
star fell on the north's edge and white birds hid
their grace in snow among the cedars' stencilled
shadows I asked for your return and twice you
came my svelte sweven blessed in transporting
black long before the red haired girl brought you
to my door—claws curled like crannied leaves
uncanny anchorage barring sky confusion stirring
the nameless distances in your eye as my home
became yours until your last—hollowed with
scapula blade under juniper and yew your grave
bleeds a geography of shy migrations beak blood
bone and bone's soul rising through sap to bole a
tree's breath delirious transpiration

here other
than wind's lamentation
nothing is

dead desert flower
for martina lowery

rain scents hawthorn and heather and her hair as
she speaks of the dead desert flower he found years
before discarded in the sinewy heat of a samarian
market its papery petals dyed the colour of dulse
and drought gifted to her with sonnets when a hare
moon stretched out over ealing—miracle plant
resurrected with each silver sparge from its glazed
ceramic tomb constant as rose gypsum on her sill
until lost after she lost him for no miracle could
survive those desolate days of condolence and dust
and yet tonight she knows a root swells as rain
brims in the cervices of his unplumbed name

cathedral
in white moonlight
birch tree

horse dream

capall bán carbon-heart and forest-veins a deep-
draped hawthorn mane we were at the fort when
hammond gave you to me finest cob ever to cut
hooves on connemara rock you stood sixteen hands
in a night whose amethyst soul we crossed—reins
luminous with insight even when you bolted on that
northern headland—lead iron splitting the ground
simpatico until you rose above a field of green stars
a laughing hallelujah my outstretched arms

the still earth
mingling with mine
a horse's breath

The Path

in a morning littered
with stars she is alone
for there is no light
in a window usually lit
by a hand unknown

quiet their passings
on a path hewn
through ash and birch
until the evening
he stopped to speak

he called her song
a poem and said
I know of you
the path alone
replied and I of you

twilighted stop
perfunctory perhaps
now silence pulsates
where a half moon
on standing water waits

spreading in this same
place each day
his crusts and crumbs
from a park bench
the drunk gardens sky

the drunk recites
a pigeon's blue clapping
wings rise

waxing moon
her swollen ankles in men's shoes
selling *The Big Issue*

wakening
in a scullery of stars
the wino folds her home

as spring hits the city
a drunk with a can
in each pocket
raises a jubilant hand
and stops the traffic

driftwood horse

through dune grass and distance a mandolin moon
lights the breast of a wild swan turning as space
closes in to wavewashed bark launched from some
well drained rooted place by axe or gale onto sea's
high altar where nude heartwood was not sick for
lack of land or for brine once beached or now for
wind scudded sand as its soul shape shifts under a
zinc roof plumed with rust and smoke one star still
in the sky as his hands guide a mare from storm
torn star bleached oak

piebald pony
tethered beside old rail tracks
silver sickle

high open ground
stippled with
silver lark song
same place where
the body was found

lowered
on lark song
his coffin

amid all
the candles
a face
I thought
was hers

the fire's scent
lingering
morning moon

river bent barely
into the gold
unknown I
have come from

rough water
waiting for the heron
evening star

dying elsewhere
in migrating moons
but at a derelict house
the blue hydrangea
blossoms wait

Aurorae

Here on the equinox's edge
the night is full of dead horses
their sedulous eyes
and magnesium hooves
soundlessly stampeding sky.
Their vaulted necks and tails
and flaming scarlet manes
their vast unfathomable souls
harnessed to the solar winds.

War Horse's Eye

Birthed at the universe's end
that star that is barely a star.
Still unnamed, astronomers say
it is colder than all others.
In a midnight carcanet
inlaid with only a glim of words
it is a war horse's clamorous eye.
White lightning-streaked sclera
dark desert iris ripe for flight.
Ending the dream a line

The war is in I

Night Driving

On the back road
out of town
there is night
blue inside bronze
hydrangea and
in a house derelict
for thirty years
there is a light.

Improper Relationship

Strangers to each other
on the outside
here he calls her wife
and she is so
for at dusk they wed
in a dark green garden
by the dementia ward.

The Crossing

In cobalt she crosses
a bridge between
two islands
where the old lay
their fallow prayers
in moon drenched
fields of hay

cervine dawn

white-lichen skinned rocks shock in their geometry
as windwarped trees like begging ballerinas im-
plore some mad god of dance and everywhere the
atlantic with each hard lapping clatters down a star-
cobbled shore while silent above it all the onyx
muzzle I approach on air moving close yet never
close enough until tensing in first light it flees and
I bereft stoop to touch a hieroglyph of leaving
touching instead a dark red heart still beating there

      cryptic love song
         her fingers in a deer's hoofprint
        at dawn

rapeseed field the dress my mother never wore

lights in a border town across the borderless bay

ochre sunset over dunes the army watchtower

headland temple ghosted in mist summer solstice

pruning a branch of stars sickle moon

white birds still on blue breaking the news

alone with a horse's shadow snow moon

all that was stolen into the dark alabaster shoulders

panthera leo leo

the architecture of proximity brooks no contact—
as I stand on the margins of this well proportioned
circle your iris distant and golden conjures
panoramic night—a gazelle's rose heart pulsing
in cinnamon wind through tamarisk and oak zeen
under toubkal unholy peak—memory trace shim-
mering skelf in a brain weary conducting corner-
less rounds of life and yet they say your role is
great you carry the blueprint of a near forgotten
race but they are not your kind reintroduction
marks a difference from before if your tiny nation
grows it will always know this endless batch of
days the myopic sun the ashlar sky the weathered
womb the crippled statuary in the dunes of your
barbary eye—eyes extinct in the wild eyes that
consider exile worse than gone forever

at the zoo
among pink clematis
lion mane

stirring places where
sad secrets bide
his words are a chrysalis
blossoming in milk
under the frozen tides

derelict house closed
for years to storms
and strangers
the emperor's wing
enters your dark chamber

harvest is done …
behind the blue hills
across bay waters
there is a field where
corn flourishes still

slipping off the sill
silver moon
and I listen
to his puppets
who never stammer

the roof of her mouth
was starless ebony
at dusk an old man
speaks of the sheepdog
he worked in his youth

wishing will not make
her fierce green eye
further gone as summer
convenes on high glass
in the palliative care ward

last time I took
the back roads south
to you I pointed out
white roses blooming
this abandoned house

even now at the dying
a feral star
in her blue borderland
illuminates politics
and the wildness of yeats

derelict house
long vanished lawns
only the magnolias
do not realise
they have gone

given to the sick
and healthy for years
before she died
her lilies stalwart still
at the road's dark side

doing it

this thinking will have to stop it is killing me as it
could have killed a man in melbourne in 1983—
with the night shift over members of the textile
workers' union punch air and faded cards—giving
our supervisor the fingers just for good measure no
malice intended nor was it ever certainly not that
morning the tiny copper-haired man appeared
beside me at the tram stop white stick tapping the
kerb's edge as the 7.15's bones rattled resplendent
in gold and green down traffic-islanded tracks only
to arrive with a glitter of grackles the thought birds
—how could he negotiate the carousel of cars? how
could I offer help without appearing condescend-
ing? no doubt he had a system a method a plan he
waited tapping while wings flapped until perplexed
by my inaction the conductor descended extending
his creased sunspangled hand—a slow release into
motion they glided over the tourmaline tar like
gene kelly and cyd charisse

diaphanous
in a hunchback moon
moth dance

haiku

guardians of small things which stop the mouth of
single sometimes sleepy seconds these poems are
made from the hollow sky-bleached bones of gold
and fire crests and willow warblers or weightless on
my palm the hibiscus kissing hummingbird that
vanished when softly the rains came

morning moon
old wound stirring
then the wren

Alzheimer's

her uncupped hands
falling water
Alzheimer's

sleepless
chaffering curtain
yelp of yellow moon

verbiage
ivy on a forgotten name
Alzheimer's

fear
warm grass
young hare's pulse

Alzheimer's
two silent shores
selfsame stars

black dog howling
in the night
insight

Alzheimer's
folding refolding
hem of her checked skirt

melancholy
cup in hollowed hands
stone cold tea

funeral
slate blue morning
crunch of gravel underfoot

black bags
her lilac blouse
the waiting wardrobe

winter grave
a star falling
through my fingers

summer sun
stomach full of butterflies
reminding myself to smile

into the night a telephone's unanswered call

                    falling from his hair
                    the rain falling
                    on her white forearm

did the poem reveal too much orchid moon?

his body language
inscrutable in blue dusk
a clambering wing

still unsure in this still night if a star died

mountain cloud
through a mare's tail
the broken blue

windward
in a mare's mane
the girl's laughter

the mare's eye
still water
stillborn prayer

white mare looming
in weed trees
old moon's shadow

morning rain
weeping under birch
mare's mane

the white mare
has foaled
faded magnolia

hard frost
under a mare's mane
her hands

twins
in memory of tony & jim mcgill

in the woods today where your son my cousin
walks the midnight dog and knows the sedge
warbler's call from snowbird and thistle finch and
wren spotting places blue jay bury acorns and
telling at a glance the under wing of kestrel merlin
peregrine and buzzard I remember the gold eyes of
a hare you rescued making your home its winter
form you kept it closer than most would perhaps
because you tasted loss earlier than others losing in
infancy half a beating rosewood heart that shining
boy your twin and later never touchstone made
of toil or money rather your mornings spent out on
the lake of an eleven month old soul and with
no footprint left on its silent shore returning to
make tea from rain and jasmine for a corn haired
daughter long after she had children of her own

headstones in mist
secrets shared
only with the dead

sounding syllables
in a name unsounded
until tonight when the hare
lowered her deep eyes
in a sapphire sky

without light he comes
through birch to speak
of verse unrevealed and
a lone owl's velvet flight
as it glances his night

did souls holy or unholy
conspire that we meet
at this time turning talk
from words to a white bird
at deserted railway lines

falling to its death
on the anniversary of hers
a star passed before we met
now in pristine dark only
the distance between

in the valley
of that first mare's eye
mourning doves
still feed on scarlet
in arizonian desert

worse things no doubt
than a horse being shot
still I wonder about
your last thought in light
bright with rowan berries

was his aim your
forehead's white star
turning supernova
as it fell among
the summer grasses?

arrested by the question
she returns to heat
and birch to follow
old horse tracks across
the earth's umber breast

horse dream

capaillín ársa was there a dream before words
pendent on lemon branch like doleful white-faced
mares in the ortolan's golden orchard? before lips
gleamed with a brattle of broken bit with a silver
insouciant *fuck it?* claretcoloured night—fingers
opaline in an avalanche of mane our only rudder
raddled with moonshine

rain on summer sand
a child writes
the dead pony's name

summer moon enshrined in shell rumours of the dead

in his black hair the bones of old prayers

seraphim on purple hills wind farm

quilted in blue moonlight the dead fox

feathering my gut with his words the rose rambles

moon clouds after dreaming her darkened hair

sign for live music echoing the blind man's stick

silver moon climbing a scaffold of stars unemployed builder

the van
in memory of sean mccotter

always a ship that ancient van you sailed from the pines
to hyacinthine horizons no scrap yard angel in the child's
eyes a brigantine barnacled with legends of rubies and
sin like the cardinal elixir firing its factious heart twenty
five years driving on red diesel and never once caught
your small rebellions so different from those of others
whose tripwire threading taffeta night mistook an old at-
lantic coloured craft for an army land rover miraculously
you survived no orange or green partitioning your
tongue resting there only a single white wafer inscribed
with *neighbour* two syllables including the boy you fed
and taught to play jack rummy after he torched your yard
stoned out of a skull hardwired that warm dusk to some
restless star your own followed each evening to a place
where glass caught light in liquid clear as siberian amber
where your one-liners were river runes—silver trout
gleaming in a mountain moon gleaming still up-anchor-
ing in morning with o'neill and mcwilliams the unfil-
tered smoke from your gallagher greens anointing a
cargo of strainers and round posts and rails the materi-
als used in the hard and honest trade you plied until
breathing your last out there on the mutinous margins
mending all the broken fences

feeding on the dregs
of summer
swallows over corn

Bird-Feeders

in memory of jo & brian mcgrath

adjusting the scarf again
chemotherapy
his wife's remains

bird-feeders on the rowan
at an open window
her coffin

all he said *her family*
and her vision - her
masterpiece unsigned

after the burial
he kneads his hands
one then the other

suspended grief
descending
first falling leaf

still in wheat-gold night an oak moth's ocelli

if only she had been buried wild crimson cyclamen

stooping on the edge of autumn purple river grass

granite hills under bracken a deer's red heart

hailstones on the blackest hair evening star

estuary mud bleached in moonlight boat bones

breaking the rose's heart a slug's winged dream

gold autumn dawn melting over fields she once owned

bronze chrysanthemums
father's old stories
retold in late autumn sun

saying *I am* after a stroke
only that storm
of lines between her eyes

pampas grass
against the purple sunset
a patient screams *enough*

the jackdaw's keen eye
somewhere
a man is shouting *nurse*

that ragged *goodbye*
echoing in the hollow
above a horse's eye

the businessman's earring

shining like a chorus among pinstripes and calvin
klein the brief case and bespoke shoes the clipped
and coiffured hair then the scent of a young
turquoise sun—trembling remnant of an aegean
season where sleep sheltering sands stirred under
cassiopeia as her dark dreams rustled in tall sea grass
the glimpse caught at his ear—leaping silver snare

single coin
in a busker's guitar case
evening star

finding my mother's orange squeezer

seventeen when I walked into a leonard cohen song
—stone and sky from judean noon to white mother-
of-pearl moon day in hills east of qalqilya that day
that did not get away the low country boughs
pendant with a thousand seedling suns at least a dirt
road hour gone from the wide silent blue where
people tend no roots then travelling blind behind
the frayed hem of a bedouin dress an old man
moves towards me through tracks left by cloven
hooves—arum lilies floating in his eyes as a daugh-
ter offers tea and oranges accepting this daughter
knows she did so endlessly before in a kitchen
bright as any lemon grove—dawn on saint mary's
casting jesus in indigo and ivory and gold as my
mother's hands found heroes among leaves and
water where there were children in the morning
leaning every morning into love as she offered tea
and oranges

amber inclusion
in the chapel's resinous air
unanswered prayer

After *La Vie En Rose*

street ballad
kohl running
on her mother's heart

        sun thronged glass
        in the brothel
        a girl gets ready for mass

clouds occlude
the full moon
her black eye patch

        beer stained table
        he recalls
        the japanese doll

roses in snow
at the saint's shrine
a young hooker

        warm café night
        the accordion player
        diverts his eyes

in blue spotlight
the singer
unfurls her hands

        remembering
        among the cacti
        an old woman

behind drapes
dusty in sunlight
a piano waits

leaving night's path
she is a moth in winter
bound for the fields
where a fire burns
of silverthorn and alder

unopened letter
haloed in lamplight
somewhere upriver
spawn song silvering
a dark salmon night

snow anointing
a harvest of old cars
as orange flames leap
from a barrel
in the breaker's yard

tonight at a manger
wise men stand silent
in the amber light
from an oxen's
weeping eye

at the hillside remains
of a stranger's fire
a stone holds heat
in the heart
of an alchemy of ashes

the timbre
of a horse's heart
winter sea

gone with the thaw
all sign among birch and stars
two paths crossed

in freezing fog
what might have been
a light

red winter roses
out there among the stars
a lapwing's cry

year's final hour
frozen leaves
a rustle of regrets

her old tracks
retraced across snow
falling silently
in a blue crystal moon
the dying year

whitebeam
in memory of sinead mcgill

planted after sinead their first girl died two days
before her birth the whitebeam seemed to know its
destiny despite loam and gravel and love and water
was not rest in that good earth rather a child's staff
in some unseen place at the edge of night—a new
constellation rising in the damson heavens

first poem
out of the blue sky
in sky blue crayon

baleen dream

thinking of his hands reciting oak they have worked
I remember the dream—forgotten until this mo-
ment a dream of baleen whales in waters they have
never seen their great unquenchable fins flung to
the scattering sun

    old prayer
        out of the dark
     echoing sea
an island

movanagher moon
in memory of willie mcgill

low over movanagher wood this new year's new
moon is a mercury quill inscribing diamond
distances in the blue baize between of day and
other as I wonder if it is a prayer or a salutation that
I offer as you offered monthly until your eighty-
fifth year unobstructed by any glass

off the gravel path
an old man's uplifted face
white lunar psalm

Glossary

Akhir an-nahr
Brightest star in the constellation Eridanus, Akhir an-nahr
is the Arabic spelling of Achernar which means End of
the River.

Andenken
German: memory, keepsake, souvenir, reminder.

Apah
Sanskrit: animate used in reference to water as a living,
breathing force.

Capall bán
Irish: white horse.

Capaillín ársa
Irish: ancient pony.

Rodden
North of Ireland dialect: track or laneway. From the Irish
'roidin' meaning a little road.

Ruuru
Australian Aboriginal language: loosely translated as
memory, reminder.

Salfay
Alphabet of Tales (1440): reward paid to the finder or restorer of old gods.

Skelf
North of Ireland dialect: splinter of wood usually embedded in skin. Also used in Scotland and in the North of England.

Souvenir
French (m): memory, recollection; memento, keepsake.

Slap
North of Ireland dialect: an opening in a hedge that is closed with a makeshift barrier rather than a conventional gate.

Thakera
Arabic: memory, souvenir.

Zikaron
Hebrew: memory, remembrance, memorial.